London

161 COLOUR ILLUSTRATIONS - MAP OF THE CITY CENTRE

Houses of Parliament.

THOMAS BENACCI LTD
LONDON

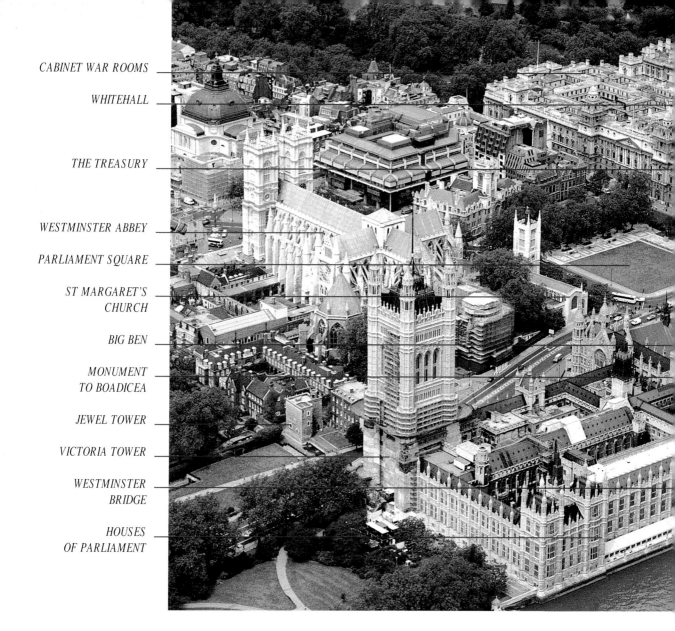

CABINET WAR ROOMS

WHITEHALL

THE TREASURY

WESTMINSTER ABBEY

PARLIAMENT SQUARE

ST MARGARET'S
CHURCH

BIG BEN

MONUMENT
TO BOADICEA

JEWEL TOWER

VICTORIA TOWER

WESTMINSTER
BRIDGE

HOUSES
OF PARLIAMENT

LONDON OVERVIEW

*How precious it is to be here, wandering ... in the
midst of the greatest city in the world, ...
Valery Larbaud, Trafalgar Square at night.*

*View of the Houses of Parliament,
Westminster Abbey and buildings along Whitehall.*

When a man is tired of London, he is
tired of life: for there is in London all
that life can afford-, wrote Samuel Johnson
in 1777. He would recognize many of the
great sights on both sides of the Thames,
which winds its way downstream from
Windsor and Hampton Court, past Westminster Abbey, St Paul's Cathedral, the Tower,
and on down to Greenwich and the sea.
When H.G. Wells wrote in 1911 that "London is
the most interesting beautiful and wonderful
city in the world to me", horse drawn carriages
and Edwardian splendour were on their way out.

The 20th century was about to enforce dramatic changes on the London skyline - skyscrapers in the City, the TelecomTower, an arts centre on the South Bank, and Docklands, the business centre for the 21st century.

Yet London, the world's capital, has kept its heart. Johnson would still be able to drink coffee in Covent Garden, or meander through the City's narrow streets to churches and livery companies with echoes of Medieval days. H.G. Wells might, today, listen to debates in the Houses of Parliament, attend a concert in the Albert Hall or listen to a military band in a royal park. Today London is a sprawling, cosmopolitan metropolis, about 1600 square km, an exciting world which many visitors from abroad see first from the sky, surprised that the ribbon-like Thames is so curvaceous and a score of bridges so decorative. Down there, over seven million people are at home, not in anonymous suburbs but in the Cities of London and Westminster and in districts which have remnants of their countrified past, in Marylebone and Kensington, Hampstead and Highgate with their own high streets and historic monuments remembering famous men and women

Portrait of Sir Winston Churchill by G. Sutherland, 1954.

who built a London which each generation discovers anew. Documented history goes back to the time when Westminster was still a marsh. The Romans had inhabited the land which became the City, building a bridge across the Thames by AD 60 and creating a celebrated centre of commerce filled with traders. Westminster, established as a royal palace shortly before the invasion of William the Conqueror in 1066, gradually grew in

London Eye.

Big Ben.

Houses of Parliament.

importance as it became the seat of government, beside the Thames and next door to Westminster Abbey a couple of minutes from the City. Big Ben, the voice of London, has been telling the time to the second since 1859. Construction of the 96 m clock tower began in the year Queen Victoria came to the throne, 1837, as part of the reconstruction of the Houses of Parliament following the devastating fire of 1834. Clock designer, Sir Edmund Grimthorpe, the architect and clockmaker all died before the 13 1/2 ton bell was mounted behind the four clock faces, which each measure 7 m in diameter.

The Great Bell cracked, was recast and cracked again, giving us the famous, flawed, resonating boom. Why Big Ben? There are two answers - either can be chosen. It could have been named after Sir Benjamin Hall, chief commissioner of works at that time, and a Welshman of great girth. Or, perhaps, it was named by workmen who brought the bell from Whitechapel Foundry on a cart pulled by 16 white horses. Their hero of the day was Benjamin Caunt, a 17 stone prize fighter.

The Sculpture of Boadicea.

*Houses of Parliament
seen from Westminster Bridge.*

Westminster Bridge, commemorative Badge.

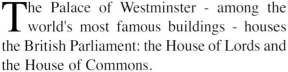

HOUSES

OF PARLIAMENT

The Palace of Westminster - among the world's most famous buildings - houses the British Parliament: the House of Lords and the House of Commons.

The first palace was built for Edward the Confessor, who came to the throne in 1042. Forty-five years later William Rufus, son of William the Conqueror, had Westminster Hall - the finest in Europe - added to the apartments and here he feasted in 1099. Henry III added the Painted Chamber in the 13th century and in his reign Parliament (from French parler - to speak or talk) had its origins. Knights from the shires and burgesses from the towns were invited to meet in 1265. Thirty years later a more democratic Model Parliament took place with representatives who were elected, not simply nominated. By 1550 the Commons and the Lords were meeting separately with Members of Parliament occupying the secularised exquisite St Stephen's Chapel.

Meanwhile the impressive Westminster Hall had been rebuilt with its hammerbeam roof and carved flying angles. When Charles II came to the throne in 1660, Cromwell's skull was stuck on a spike on the roof, where it rotted for 25 years. By the 19th century overcrowding had become a major problem.

London Eye at night.

Houses of Parliament.

Plans for rebuilding were hastened in dramatic fashion when the night skies of London were lit up with a fierce blaze. The Palace of Westminster was engulfed in a fire in 1834. Sir Charles Barry received the commission to build anew, in Gothic splendour, with the assistance of Augustus Pugin who provided picturesque ornamentation. St Stephen's Chapel became St Stephen's Hall - a wide corridor with paintings and marble sculptures and a brass stud on the floor marking where the Speaker's chair used to stand.

The crypt survived, so did Westminster Hall, although the neighbouring chamber of the Commons was destroyed yet again, in the Second World War. Every British citizen has the traditional right to ask to see his or her Member of Parliament, and they meet in the highly decorative Central Lobby. When Parliament is sitting, it is possible to hear debates from the Strangers' Galleries. Even the Queen is subject to restrictions. For the State Opening of Parliament she has to sit enthroned in the Lords while the Prime Minister and the Cabinet are summoned from the Commons - a custom which goes back to the era of Charles I, who burst in, demanding the arrest of five Members of Parliament. He failed.

7

HOUSE OF LORDS
HOUSE OF COMMONS

Houses of Parliament. Central Lobby.

Houses of Parliament. The House of Lords.

Until recently the House of Lords was composed of senior Anglican bishops and titled hereditary peers who were appointed for life as a right of birth. Although the bishops, or the Lords Spiritual, as they are known, remain, new legislation has restricted the number of hereditary peers to only 90, elected by the House from the hereditary peers.

In the Chamber - where State Openings of Parliament take place with the Queen reading from the throne - the Lord Chancellor, who is also Speaker, has a seat called the Woolsack, formerly made of a large sack of wool. The Lord Chancellor is the highest civil subject in the land and takes precedence, after the royal family, before all the Queen's other subjects, with the exception of the Archbishop of Canterbury. On either side of the Peers' Corridor frescoes depict events of the 17th century, including King Charles I's intrusion into the House of Commons in 1642. The average attendance at the House of Lords, which sits on about 140 days a year is 270, but in the course of a year some 800 partake in the proceedings. The official report of Parliament's business is called Hansard. Parliament's paramount power is to make laws. It provides, through taxation, the means to govern, a democratic process

Background. Westminster Hall.

ensured by the party system which provides each government with an Opposition. Parliament consists of two chambers - the House of Lords and the Commons with 650 elected members.

Beyond the Central Lobby is the Members' Lobby, so called because only lobby correspondents can accompany Members this far. Beyond here are the Aye and No Lobbies where Members pass through for a count when a vote or Division is called during debate. In the main chamber, the Speaker presides with the symbol of his authority, the Mace, on the table. The Prime Minister and Government Ministers sit on the front bench on the right side. The Opposition are on the left side.

For relaxation, the Members of Parliament have reception rooms which lead onto the riverside terrace. That could not be used until 1865 when London's new sewerage system opened and reduced the stink from the polluted Thames. In gardens across the road is the Jewel Tower, a stone structure built in 1365 to 66 as a royal treasure house. Among modern sculptures to have been placed in the vicinity is a masterpiece by Sir Henry Moore, while Sir Winston Churchill presides over Parliament Square, with his larger-than-life size sculpture raised on a plinth.

Houses of Parliament. St. Stephen's Hall.

Houses of Parliament. The House of Commons.

ELIZABETH I (1533-1603)

Queen of England and Ireland, she was born at Greenwich Palace, the only child of Henry VIII and Anne Boleyn. The Spanish ambassador remarked that "she gives her orders and has her way as absolutely as her father did". She kept close personal control over councillors, parliament, foreign policy, religion and was a leader in critical moments. In her speech before the troops at Tilbury, on August 8, 1588, with invasion imminent from The Netherlands, she said:"My loving people... I know I have the body of a weak and feeble woman, but I have the heart and stomach of a king, and of a king of England too".

Portrait of Queen Elizabeth I. Unknown artist c. 1575.

WESTMINSTER ABBEY

The wonders of Westminster Abbey owe much to a succession of kings and queens beginning with Edward the Confessor, a saintly man who came to the throne in 1040. Sadly the church he built on the site was consecrated on December 28, 1065 when he was too weak to attend. He died eight days later. The next year a new king, William the Conqueror was crowned there on Christmas Day setting a precedent which continues. Westminster Abbey has been the setting for every monarch's coronation and, since 1308, they have used the Coronation

Westminster Abbey. Facade.

Westminster Abbey. Nave looking East.

Westminster Abbey. Henry VII's Chapel
Westminster Abbey. Henry VII's Chapel. Ceiling.

Westminster Abbey. Choir, High Altar and Apse.
Westminster Abbey. Coronation Chair.

Chair designed to hold the ancient Stone of Scone seized from the Scots in 1296. It was stolen by some Scots in 1950 but replaced the following year, and in 1996 was given back to the Scots. Henry III added a Lady Chapel in 1220 and began rebuilding the old Abbey - a process which lasted some 300 years to create most of the building we know today - though the West Towers were not finished until 1745. The Abbey presents a pageant of noble, military, political and artistic history. It has the graves of kings and queens, of poets (Chaucer was the first to be buried, in 1400, in Poets' Corner), politicians and churchmen. Sir Winston Churchill is remembered with a marble slab placed near the tomb of the Unknown Warrior. Elizabeth I is buried in the same vault as her half-sister, Mary, and is portrayed in a white marble effigy. She lies in the north aisle of the Henry VII chapel, under its spectacular vaulted roof. The damaged shrine in the chapel behind the High Altar still contains the body of Edward the Confessor, the Abbey's founder. Westminster Abbey, under the jurisdiction of a Dean and Chapter, is subject only to the Sovereign. It has its own choir and choir school and adjoining the cloisters is Westminster School, founded by Queen Elizabeth I.

HENRY VIII (1491-1547)

King of England and Ireland he personifies the transition from the Middle Ages to modern times. He succeeded in unifying the country, in abolishing papal jurisdiction and obtaining what he desired from Parliament. He may be remembered for the birth of the English naval power, the dissolution of the monasteries and the death penalty for wives and friends.

Portrait of Henry VIII by Unknown artist c.1520.

View of Whitehall.

Banqueting House

AROUND WHITEHALL

Downing Street, the official residence of Prime Ministers for more than 250 years, was built on land where an Abbey brewhouse had been sited. During restoration over 40 years ago, remnants of Roman pottery were unearthed, along with Saxon wood and fragments of Whitehall Palace which had its heyday during the reign of Tudor Henry VIII. The famous cul-de-sac of Downing Street was created by Sir George Downing, Member of Parliament, around 1680. He had spent his early years with his parents in America and became a graduate of Harvard University before returning to London and winning the approval of Charles II, who granted him a lease on the land. Number 10 is one of the original Downing Street houses to survive.

Acquired by the Crown in 1732, it was offered by George II as a gift to Sir Robert Walpole. He accepted it in his office as First Lord of the Treasury (a title which eventually became 'Prime Minister'). Among famous incumbents was Sir Robert Peel, who formed the police force - hence the nick-name 'bobbies'.

No. 10, with the most photographed door in the world, is guarded outside by a single policeman. It has seen the most significant comings and goings of each era from riots to suffragettes chaining themselves to the railings to Sir Winston Churchill's celebration at the end of the War. In recent years it has witnessed the arrival of the first female Prime Minister, Mrs Margaret Thatcher. No.11 is the residence of the Chancellor of the Exchequer and No.12 is the office of the Chief Whip, whose job is to ensure Members of Parliament toe the party line.

No. 10 Downing Street.

Whitehall. The Cenotaph.

In 1990, for security reasons, a pair of gates was erected at the end of the street. Downing Street leads into Whitehall, home of government ministries and the setting for state processions, and for the annual memorial services at the Cenotaph. This was designed by Sir Edwin Lutyens to remember the dead of the First World War, with an inscription added after the Second World War. Nearby, Charles I was executed in 1649, having walked out from the Banqueting Hall, built 24 years earlier of Portland stone in Palladian architecture by Inigo Jones. The ceiling celebrates the reign of his father, James I, and in particular, the union of England and Scotland. Among the allegorical scenes are depictions of the birth and coronation of the unfortunate king. Cromwell's commonwealth with him as Protector lasted a decade. The Monarchy returned with Charles II in 1660.

Whitehall and Big Ben seen from Trafalgar Square.

Horse Guard.

Kings Troop Royal Horse Artillery.

H.M. Queen Elizabeth II leaving for the State Opening of Parliament.

Trooping the Colour.

Whitehall. Trooping the Colour.

CEREMONIES AND PARADES

Welsh Guard.

WELLINGTON ARCH

QUEEN'S AUDIENCE
CHAMBER

THE THRONE ROOM

THE PICTURE
GALLERY

THE STATE DINING
ROOM

THE STATE BALL-
ROOM

BUCKINGHAM
PALACE

QUEEN VICTORIA (1819-1901)

Queen of the United Kingdom of Great Britain and Ireland, and from 1876 Empress of India, she was tenacious, obstinate, and delighted in ceremonies and etiquette. She married Prince Albert in 1840. After their marriage, life at court quickly changed. She had nine children. In politics she established an intelligence service abroad and governed with talent. Her long reign contributed to establish a "democratic monarchy" and to consolidate the Monarchy itself.

Portrait of Queen Victoria by Sir George Hayter, 1838.

Buckingham Palace and the Monument to Queen Victoria.

Buckingham Palace, gate.

Changing of the Guard

Buckingham Palace, gate.

Queen Victoria monument.

ADMIRALTY ARCH

A dmiralty Arch stands at the entrance to the Mall, which leads down to Buckingham Palace. It was designed by Sir Aston Webb as a memorial to Queen Victoria. The central gate is usually closed as only the sovereign may pass through it.

Buckingham Palace, facing The Mall and the white marble and gilded Queen Victoria Memorial, flies the royal standard when the Queen is in residence. Her ancestor, King George IV, insisted that the architect for his stately new home must be John Nash. He won his choice, but the cost grew to a horrendous £ 700,000, when extravagances included such items as 500 massive blocks of veined Carrara marble. When Queen Victoria came to the throne a few years later in 1837 it was hardly habitable. Many of the 1,000 windows would not open. By 1853 the ballroom

block had been added. King Edward VII, born in the Palace in 1841, died there in 1910.

Despite its sumptuous apartments, containing generations of royal treasures, not all its residents were happy. In his memoirs the Duke of Windsor wrote that the vast building "with its stately rooms and endless corridors and passages, seemed pervaded by a curious, musty smell that still assails me whenever I enter its portals".

Today the Queen and the Duke of Edinburgh have private suites in the North Wing, overlooking Green Park. Their home is open to around 30,000 guests in summer, attending garden parties. The State Apartments, which contain many treasures, are now open to the public in the months of August and September. In summer 2011 more than 600,000 members of the public visited Buckingham Palace to view the dress that Kate Middleton wore on her wedding day to Prince William.

Buckingham Palace is a working setting for the monarchy - with a large staff involved in tasks from running the household to organising banquets for visiting heads of state, arrangements for ambassadors to present their credentials and subjects to receive awards. From here the Queen leaves on ceremonial duties such as the State Opening of Parliament in early winter and Trooping the Colour to mark her official birthday in June.

The Queen's Gallery, built on part of the site where the chapel stood before it was bombed during the war, houses changing exhibitions taken from the Royal Collections. This is open to the public. So are the Royal Mews with the Queen's horses, their trappings, the breathtaking State Coach, painted by Cipriani, and more modern royal carriages and cars.

Carlton House Terrace.

Parade down The Mall.

Admiralty Arch.

ROYAL

RESIDENCES

Clarence House.

St James's Palace.

Some of today's Royals reside in Kensington Palace in Kensington Gardens. The first royal residents were William III and Queen Mary, who bought Nottingham House in the village of Kensington for £18,000 in 1689. This was their country mansion, just outside the less healthy Westminster, and they asked Sir Christopher Wren to make necessary improvements. Thus Kensington expanded, and is still known as a royal borough.

The State Apartments were opened to the public in 1899 by Queen Victoria who was born and brought up there. Today the Palace is the setting for a glamorous Court Dress Collection, showing the fashions in vogue during two centuries.

St James's Palace, an irregular, picture-pretty brick building was created by Henry VIII. The gatehouse, parts of the Chapel Royal and the Tapestry Room survive from the 16th century, much as they were when Mary I died here in 1558. Charles I spent his last days at this

Background. The Imperial State Crown.

24

Hampton Court Palace.

Palace, and since then, happier royal connections continued. The Duke and Duchess of Kent live in a grace and favour residence, the Lord Chamberlain has offices and the British Court is still called the Court of St James.

Clarence House situated 200 mts from Buckingham Palace, along the Mall, for many years the residence of the former Queen Mother was built by John Nash in 1825 for William IV when he was Duke of Clarence. It is adjacent to St James's Palace.

The Queen lived here as Princess Elizabeth after her marriage, and the Princess of Wales spent days here before her marriage.

Marlborough House was built for Sarah, Duchess of Marlborough who obtained a lease on land adjoining St James's Palace from Queen Anne. The house, completed in 1711, was the birthplace of the future George V in 1865. Nearly 100 years later the House was donated to the Government as a Commonwealth Centre.

Windsor Castle.

WESTMINSTER

CATHEDRAL

Westminster Cathedral - seat of the Cardinal Archbishop, and the leading Roman Catholic Church in England, was built at the turn of the century near Victoria Station, half a mile from the Abbey. The single bell in the 280 foot high campanile is dedicated (like the Chapel in the Abbey) to Edward the Confessor. This gift from Gwendolen, Duchess of Norfolk, is inscribed "St Edward, pray for England".

Westminster Cathedral.

Westminster Cathedral. The nave, East end.   *Westminster Cathedral. Lady Chapel.*

Three hundred years elapsed after the Reformation until government by diocesan bishops was restored to Roman Catholics in Britain. The first Archbishop of Westminster, Cardinal Wiseman, was appointed in 1850 but another generation elapsed until, in 1884, the site was acquired: this had been a former marshland which became a market used by the Benedictine monks of the Abbey.

The Cathedral, designed by J.F. Bentley was built in Early Christian Byzantine style between 1895 and 1903, composed of red brick with bands of grey Portland stone. More than 100 different kinds of marbles from quarries worldwide were used for interior decoration. Eight dark green marble columns, which line the widest nave in England, arrived in 1899 having been delayed for two years when they were seized as spoils of war by Turks during transportation across Thessaly.

The 14 stations of the Cross are carved in stone in low relief by Eric Gill. An early 15th century alabaster statue of Our Lady and Child, from the Nottingham School, was presented by an anonymous donor, while the marble pulpit was the gift of Cardinal Bourne in 1934. The Tower Viewing Gallery can be visited providing spectacular views of London. The Cathedral, which is said to contain some fragments of the True Cross, has chapels to commemorate St Thomas of Canterbury, St George and the English Martyrs, and saints of Ireland and Scotland.

A novel feature is the organ which can be played from either end of the Cathedral. This was the setting for the first London performance of Sir Edward Elgar's Dream of Gerontius, which the composer conducted in 1903.

Royal Albert Hall

THE GREAT EXHIBITION 1851

Albert Memorial.

Royal Albert Hall and Albert Memorial.

Prince Albert suggested that the profits from the 1851 Great Exhibition should pay for new museums, libraries, schools and exhibition rooms. He died 10 years later - before plans for a grand concert hall reached fruition. Difficulties, including shortage of cash meant that Queen Victoria didn't lay the foundation stone of the Royal Albert Hall until 1868 (this is in position behind block K at the rear of the stalls). Two years later the Prince of Wales declared the Hall open. It is oval, with a capacity for 7,000 under a glass and iron dome 135 feet high internally. On the outside a frieze illustrates the Triumph of Arts and Letters. Wagner conducted the Wagner festival concerts here in 1877 but the Hall, with its organ containing nearly 9,000 pipes and improved acoustics, is now best known as the home of Sir Henry Wood's Promenade Concerts - simply called The Proms. Opposite the Royal Albert Hall, in Hyde Park is the Albert Memorial designed by George Gilbert Scott (knighted for his skills). The style

South Bank Arts Complex.

is high Victorian Gothic with seven tiers of statuary -an extraordinarily elaborate work of art which was almost complete in 1872. The 14 foot high bronze statue of the Prince holding the catalogue of the Great Exhibition by John Foley was installed in 1876.

Exactly 100 years after the Great Exhibition, the Festival of Britain swept aside post-war austerity and the Royal Festival Hall on the South Bank became a central focus. Around the spacious concert Hall a flourishing arts centre is to be found, with the Queen Elizabeth Hall, Purcell Room, Hayward Gallery, National Theatre, and BFI Southbank which houses a remarkable centre celebrating film and archive footage. The Barbican is the largest performing arts centre in Europe and plays host to world class touring theatre companies and is also the home of both the London Symphony Orchestra and the BBC Symphony Orchestra.

The former Planetarium, now the Marvel Superheroes 4D attraction and Madame Tussauds

Mme Tussauds. King Henry VIII with his wives.

Portrait of Arthur Wellesley by Robert Home 1804.

ARTHUR WELLESLEY, IST **DUKE OF WELLINGTON (1769-1852)**
The"Iron Duke" was the general who faced Napoleon's armies all over Europe, and particularly in Portugal and Spain, until their final defeat at Waterloo. He was considered the hero of the Victorian epoch; he lived in Apsley House -now a museum of his war trophies- at N°1 London.

FROM MME TUSSAUDS
TO HYDE PARK CORNER

At Madame Tussauds in Marylebone visitors mingle with the famous and infamous, with the royal family, pop stars, and in the Chamber of Horrors meet executioners at work in lurid reality. The founder, born as Marie Grosholtz, came face to face with death. As a waxworker of renown in Paris and former art tutor to the sister of Louis XVI, she was

Wellington House.

commanded by the leaders of the French Revolution to take death masks from the decapitated heads of the victims of the guillotine. Having married a civil engineer, François Tussaud, she came to London early in the 19th century and by the time of her death in 1850 at the age of 89, her waxworks were famous. Her grandson, Joseph Randall Tussaud, supervised their move to the present site near Baker Street in 1884 since when the collection has kept pace with society - good, evil, stately - and stars. Next door is the former London Planetarium with its green copper dome; it was opened by the Duke of Edinburgh in 1958. Since 2010 it has housed the Marvel 4D Superhero attraction and is part of the Madame Tussauds museum dedicated to famous persons.

Marble Arch designed by John Nash in 1827, based on the Arch of Constantine in Rome, was moved from outside Buckingham Palace to its present site in 1851 - the year of the Great Exhibition. It marks the North East corner of Hyde Park, near where anyone can take a stand and address anyone else who will listen - hence its name: Speakers' Corner.

Hyde Park Corner, at the far end of the elegant Park Lane, has another arch - Wellington Arch - dating from the 1820s. Next door is Apsley House, the home of the Duke of Wellington (1769-1852) with the distinguished address, No.1 London, and a suitably distinguished collection of porcelain, paintings and personal relics of the Iron Duke.

Wellington Arch.

Marble Arch.

THE PARKS OF LONDON

Green Park.

The Royal Parks of London - St James's, Green Park, Hyde Park, Kensington Gardens and Regent's Park - are central London's lungs. Bands play beside lakes; they have cafes and art galleries. Riders trot around Rotten Row; oarsmen row boats across the Serpentine and in summer players take to the stage at the Regent's Park Open Air Theatre.

Although deer no longer live here, the bird life is prolific, encouraged by sanctuaries. The one in St James's is nicely sited on Duck Island where pelicans first made their home in the 17th century - a pair were given as a gift by the Russian ambassador - and King Charles II brought his aviary here.

Kensington Gardens, with its sunken gardens, orangery and the Round Pond - joy of children with small sailing boats - gained its early character in the days of William III, who lived in Kensington Palace. Queen Caroline, wife of George II, made substantial changes, planting avenues of trees and building ornate architectural features. Beside the Serpentine is the nursery-book statue of Peter Pan, based on the much beloved fictitious character created by Sir James Barrie at the turn of the 20th century. South of the Serpentine you will also find the Diana, Princess of Wales memorial fountain opened in 2004 to commemorate the late princess.

Kew Gardens. The Palm House.

In Hyde Park 41 gun salutes celebrate the Sovereign's birthday, lovers stroll and fireworks are let off on special occasions and, in early November, historical cars begin their London to Brighton run.

In Regent's Park favourite venues are a miniature garden on an island, Queen Mary's Rose Gardens, a long wide avenue, ornate sculptures and open grounds for sports, and for dogs to run free in sight of inhabitants of the London Zoo. Although most of the bigger show stopping animals have now been removed from the zoo, it still sponsors important conservation projects and remains a fascinating London attraction.

Hyde Park.

HORATIO NELSON, VISCOUNT NELSON (1758-1805)
His rapid rise to the admiralty was mainly due to the respect he showed for his captains. He had the honour of leading his fleet against the French in a series of campaigns, and at Trafalgar the 21st October 1805 he defeated them. In his speech to the crew before this battle he said: "England expects that every man will do his duty". Nelson died of his wounds. He is buried in St Paul's Cathedral, in London.

Portrait of Horatio Nelson by Sir William Beechey, 1800.

National Gallery.

Trafalgar Square, Nelson's Column.

FROM PICCADILLY

TO TRAFALGAR SQUARE

Piccadilly Circus was formed in 1819 at the intersection of Piccadilly and the fashionable Regent Street, whose gracious curve was modernised with new facades 70 years ago. The Circus is a popular meeting place for both Londoners and visitors and at night is enlivened by many illuminated advertisments. On the south side is the famous statue of Eros, really the Angel of Christian Charity. The aluminium sculpture is properly titled the Shaftesbury Memorial, having been wrought by Sir Alfred Gilbert in 1892-3 as a tribute to the Earl of Shaftesbury, a Victorian Philanthropist. In Trafalgar Square, Nelson stands atop his 145 foot high monument. This legendary admiral, victor of the Battle of Trafalgar 1805, and here poised on a classical column, is guarded by a quartet of lions modelled by Sir Edwin Landseer and cast by Marocchetti in 1867. Four bronze reliefs near the base are cast from French cannon captured at the naval battles they illustrate. Trafalgar Square, with the National Gallery on the North Side and Whitehall to the South, is frequented as much by pigeons as by people. A Christmas tree is sent as a gift each year from Norway and on New Year's Eve crowds gather around the tree and the lions to herald in the new year.

Piccadilly Circus.

Trafalgar Square.

Soho

Covent Garden

S oho, the home of strip-tease, the cinema industry and international haute cuisine, is on the edge of theatreland, rich in history and rich in cultural mix. The name Soho probably came from an ancient hunting cry - So-Ho - in its farmland days. Among the earliest residents of this increasingly cosmopolitan heart of London was Charles II's illegitimate son, the Duke of Monmouth. By the 19th century it must have seemed a strange area, described by John Galsworthy in the Forsyte Saga as "Untidy, full of Greeks, Ishmaelites, cats, Italians, tomatoes, restaurants, organs, coloured stuffs, queer names, people looking out of upper windows, it dwells remote from the British Body Politic". Today there's a complete China town and restaurants serve haute cuisine from scores of countries.

Berwick Street market provides the best displays of fresh fruit and vegetables, while clubs present a saucier frontage. Soho is for shopping, entertainment and browsing or dining day and night.

Chinatown.

Chinatown Gerrard Street.

Covent Garden.

Covent Garden, a fascinating short walk away, was once pastureland belonging to the Abbey at Westminster. In the 17th century the Fourth Earl of Bedford summoned Inigo Jones and the continental style Piazza was born, complete with St Paul's Church and then a market which Hogarth portrayed in engravings. The area went downhill - Turkish baths and brothels thrived until, in the 19th century, Charles Fowler designed a smart new market. Fashionable Londoners now mingled with farmers, costermongers, and flower girls who inspired Pygmalion, which became the musical My Fair Lady.

Times change: the Flower Market is now London Transport Museum and the main buildings have been transformed into shops and restaurants in the years since the fresh produce moved to more spacious accommodation in Nine Elms, just South West of Vauxhall Bridge.

Covent Garden Opera House, home of the Royal Opera and Royal Ballet companies is actually the third theatre on the site, designed by E.M. Barry in 1858 and enlarged in the 1990's. In early years moments of unintentional drama ranged from riots in 1763 when entry at half price after the third act was refused and in 1833 when the famous actor Edmund Kean had a stroke during a performance of Othello. The present Opera House is noted for its lavish productions with the world's finest performers.

THE THAMES

Sweet Thames, run softly, till I end my song

T.S. Eliot. III. The Fire Sermon
(The Waste Land)

The Thames, described variously as "liquid history" and the "noblest river in Europe" is graced in London with a score of bridges, tunnels and a barrier, but until 1750, when the first Westminster Bridge opened, London Bridge was the one and only. The first one built in stone from 1176 to 1209 became renowned throughout Europe for its houses and a chapel dedicated to St Thomas of Canterbury. Decapitated heads of traitors were stuck on spikes on fortified gates. While the dismantled 1823-31 bridge, built by Sir John Rennie, was re-erected at Lake Havasu City, Arizona a new one was installed made of pre-stressed concrete cantilevers. Several of London's bridges have special features - Hammersmith Bridge has ornamental metal work and Vauxhall has larger than life bronze figures representing pottery, engineering, architecture, agriculture, science, fine arts, local government and education. Among the boats which ply the river, few attract more attention than the Oxford and Cambridge University Boat Race. One of London's most unusual riverside monuments is the Peace Pagoda built in Battersea Park (on the far side from Chelsea) by Buddhist monks. The double roofed pagoda, 110 feet high is part of an international chain of peace.

Old Royal Naval College, Greenwich.

The Millennium Bridge with St Paul's Cathedral in the background.

Cleopatra's Needle.

Canary Wharf. Docklands.

London Eye.

ST PAUL'S
CATHEDRAL

St. Paul's Cathedral. Interior.

St Paul's Cathedral, the seat of the Bishop of London and the spiritual centre of the City, is Sir Christopher Wren's masterpiece. He supervised its building from across the river, in a house from which he could watch his magnum opus arise on a prominent position at the top of Ludgate Hill. His mammoth achievement took 35 years to create beginning soon after the Fire of London in 1666 during which the older church - ravaged by the Parliamentary army in the 1650s - was finally destroyed.

The Cathedral, a fitting setting for the marriage of Prince Charles and Princess Diana in 1981, has the grandeur of scale with a nave 574 feet long and a height of 365 feet from the floor to the top of the cross. It also has artistic sensitivity, from Grinling Gibbons' immaculate carvings to frescoes of scenes from the life of St Paul painted by Sir James Thornhill on the inner dome.

The paintings can be seen from the Whispering Gallery 100 feet above floor level. St Paul's was the burial place of Wren, who died at the age of 91, having changed London's skyline with some 50 exquisite churches. His tomb, one of the first in the Cathedral, is marked by a black marble slab in the crypt.

St Paul's is the resting place of Admiral Lord Nelson and the Duke of Wellington. While it has witnessed sombre funeral processions, the bell called Great Tom is generally only tolled for the deaths of members of the royal family, bishops of London, deans of St Paul's and the Lord Mayor of London, should he or she die in office.

The old churchyard is a public garden. Remnants of the medieval cloister are visible and a memorial marks the approximate site of St Paul's Cross, an open air pulpit where the Pope's condemnation of Martin Luther was proclaimed in the presence of Cardinal Wolsey. Near here some of the Gunpowder Plot conspirators were hanged, having failed to blow up the Houses of Parliament.

In more peaceful vein in Paternoster Square is Elizabeth Frink's 1975 sculpture of a shepherd and sheep.

St Paul's Cathedral. The Dome seen from Millennium Bridge.

St Paul's Cathedral. South side.

THE CITY OF LONDON

The Monument.　　　　　　　　　　　　　　　　　　　　*Bank of England.*

Where the City of London stands the Romans formed a settlement nearly 2,000 years ago. By AD 200 it was protected with a wall, following attack by the tribe of Iceni, led by Queen Boadicea. Sections of the wall survive. Four hundred years later in 604 the first Bishop of London, Mellitus, began building a church dedicated to St Paul, but turbulence continued in the form of Danish invasions and then the arrival of William the Conqueror from France. A charter acknowledging citizens' rights under his reign is preserved in the Guildhall. That became the centre of civic government and was used for important trials.

Lady Jane Grey was tried here with her husband, Lord Guildford Dudley, in 1553 and in the same year Archbishop Cranmer was tried, released, only to be burned at the stake three years later. The medieval building, damaged in the 1666 fire, was rebuilt by Wren and nearly 200 years later, in 1862, it was decided to erect an open (rather than a flat) roof in sympathy with the original medieval design. That was damaged in the Second World War since when restoration continued with the creation of a new Livery Hall. The Bank of England was founded on a revolutionary idea of a national debt enabling the Government to raise money "upon a Fund of Perpetual Interest". In 1694 the Bank of England Act was passed to raise money for the French-Dutch war. The debt had risen to £ 36 million by 1715 and the institution, of increasing importance, moved to Threadneedle Street in 1734. By 1788 it was reconstructed with a neoclassical building, surrounded by a windowless wall designed by Sir John Soane. The present building, retaining Soane's curtain wall, was built by Sir Herbert Baker from 1925-39. In 1946 the Bank came into public ownership. It is now the government bank advising on monetary policy and issuing the country's bank-notes. The first Royal Exchange was built in the 16th century as a trading centre by Sir Thomas Gresham. The present building, the third on the site, was opened by Queen Victoria in 1844. On the top of the campanile is a grasshopper, Gresham's emblem.

The City of London.

The London Crest.

CITY CEREMONIES

The Lord Mayor's Show in November is the highlight of City pageantry, taking place on the second Saturday in November, the day after the new Lord Mayor is sworn into office. He or she (the first woman Lord Mayor was Lady Donaldson, serving from 1983-4) must have spent years with the City Corporation, and have enough personal wealth to host banquets at the official residence, Mansion House. The Palladian mansion was built in the 18th century with ball-room and banqueting room (known as the Egyptian Hall, with columns on all sides and clerestory above).

During the Lord Mayor's Show the new Lord Mayor goes to swear his oath of loyalty to the sovereign at the Royal Courts of Justice (Law Courts) in the Strand, just outside the City boundary. The Law Courts were built in the Gothic style in the 19th century, to hear civil, non-criminal cases.

Criminal cases are heard at the Central Criminal Court, commonly called the Old Bailey after a local street, in a 1907 edifice on the site of the ill-reputed Newgate Prison. Atop the roof is a bronze sculpture of Justice with scales and sword: she is not blindfolded.

The City police force is the only one not under the direct control of the Home Secretary. And how to spot the difference? These policemen have crested helmets and gold buttons.

The Bank of England and the Royal Exchange.

Royal Courts of Justice.

Lord Mayor of the City of London.

The Lloyds building by Richard Rogers.

TOWER
OF LONDON
TOWER BRIDGE

MARTIN TOWER

BRICK TOWER

BOWYER TOWER

WATERLOO BARRACKS
(CROWN JEWELS)

WHITE TOWER

DEVEREUX TOWER

ST PETER'S CHAPEL

BEAUCHAMP TOWER

BLOODY TOWER

WAKEFIELD TOWER

QUEEN'S HOUSE

BELL TOWER

TRAITORS' GATE

BYWARD TOWER

Beefeaters.

Portrait of Sir Thomas More. Hans Holbein, 1527.

SIR THOMAS MORE (1478-1535)
*He was born in Milk Street in the City of London and lived in Chelsea.
A celebrated philosopher, he was esteemed by everyone and favoured
by King Henry VIII, who used to visit him at home.
More, in the end, refused to recognize the Sovereign as head of the
Church and was imprisoned in the Tower and later beheaded.*

Tower Bridge

Ceremony of the Keys (Det.).

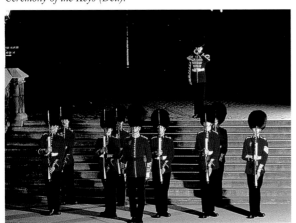

Tower of London. The White Tower.

The Tower of London has been "fortress, palace, home of the Crown Jewels and national treasures, arsenal, mint, prison, observatory, zoo and tourist attraction", wrote the Duke of Edinburgh in a book celebrating the Tower's 900th anniversary.

During its earliest days royalty lived in the secure White Tower, with walls up to 15 feet thick, but from the reign of Henry III these apartments were between Tower and River. The Traitor's Gate, the river entry, summons up the vision of distinguished prisoners entering, doomed to die - from Sir Walter Raleigh, imprisoned for 13 years to Queen Anne Boleyn. But the future Elizabeth I was released - to become Queen.

In the days of the Reformation harsh treatment became normal

A Beefeater.

Imperial State Crown. Coronation bracelets. Queen's Sceptre surmounted by a seagull made for Mary II. Royal Sceptre. The Sword of State.

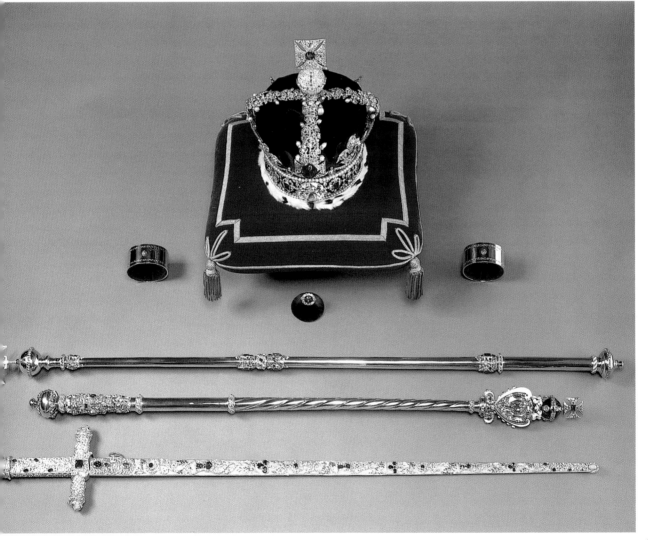

and the sufferings of those incarcerated are well documented. The old crown jewels were dismantled, but following the return of kings, the Stuart dynasty supervised the initial concept of a national museum commemorating the military achievement of king and country, and with the royal armories.

The royal menagerie departed to the Zoo in 1834, leaving only the ravens behind. Tradition says that if the ravens leave, the Tower and the country will fall. Today, neither palace nor prison, the Tower maintains elements of tradition, from the uniform of Beefeater to the nightly Ceremony of the Keys acted out by the Chief Yeoman Warder in long red cloak and Tudor bonnet, and carrying a lantern on his approach to the Bloody Tower.

The Crown Jewels are mostly post-Cromwel-

City Hall.

Tower Bridge.

HMS Belfast passing through Tower Bridge.

lian though the oldest objects survive from previous centuries: they are used in the most sacred moments during the coronation and include the anointing spoon, thought to be late 12th century and the Ampulla, which holds the holy oil, probably used at the coronation of Henry IV in 1399. St. Edward 's Crown, nearly five pounds in weight, was made for the Coronation of Charles II in 1661.The Imperial State Crown (1838) contains the Black Prince's ruby. Tower Bridge was opened in 1894, built in the Gothic style to blend in with the nearby Tower of London. The bascules, weighing 1,000 tons each, are now operated by electricity, and will open to let ships pass through, though much less frequently than in the past. The original

hydraulic machinery can now be seen in the museum, and it is also possible to cross the overhead walkways, which offer fine views.

St Katharine Docks, 23 acres between London Docks and the Tower has a new lease of life - as a tourist attraction with a marina, a collection of old Thames barges, shops and a pub, the Dickens Inn. The powerful Second World War cruiser HMS Belfast is moored in the River. From the early 1820s the Docks were full of sailing vessels returning from around the world, with cargoes of ivory, marble, wool, rubber, wine and tea, but as larger ships moored downriver, her docks and warehouses fell into disrepair. Today they have, as replacements, the Hilton Canary Wharf and the Tower Thistle Hotel.

WILLIAM SHAKESPEARE (1564-1616)

He was born at Stratford-upon-Avon; his life is practically unknown until 1592 when we meet him in London as actor and playwright. Elizabethan London was certainly crowded and noisy and Shakespeare captured the spirit which inspired his comedies. After the reopening of the theatres in 1594, having been closed during the Plague, it appears he wrote two comedies a year. In London he lived in Southwark, in Bishopsgate and with the reopening of the Globe Theatre, in Cripplegate. Shakespeare wrote 37 plays, among which Romeo and Juliet, Hamlet, Othello, The Tempest, Macbeth. He has been defined "The world's best known poet".

Portrait of William Shakespeare by John Taylor.

THEATRES

Shakespeare's Theatre rebuilt.

Theatre Royal Haymarket.
Royal Opera House.
The audience at the Globe.

Roll up! Roll up! Audiences have crowded into the Palladium since it opened as a music hall in 1910. London's theatres have drawn attention for unrivalled standards ever since the days of Shakespeare when his plays were enacted in the Globe Theatre.

Drury Lane, Shaftesbury Avenue, Haymarket and the Novello Theatre are bright with theatrical lights, with musicals and dramas, farce and comedy. Theatre isn't confined to the West End: the stages of the Royal Court in Sloane Square, the Barbican in the City and the National Theatre on the South Bank beckon nightly. Fringe theatre has been growing but with an ever changing choice of productions to see, for longevity there's nothing to beat Agatha Christie's The Mousetrap, which runs and runs.

MUSEUMS
AND GALLERIES

British Museum. Parthenon Frieze. Sculptures by Phidias.

The Royal Academy of Arts.

The National Gallery. Sainsbury Wing.

The National Gallery was born when King George IV urged the government to purchase a collection of 38 paintings including six of Hogarth's Marriage à la Mode. Rubens, Rembrandt, other Flemish, Dutch and Italian Renaissance masters were acquired as years passed and the Gallery grew, and is still growing as a mecca of world class paintings. Next door is the National Portrait Gallery, one of the first major institutions to acknowledge the importance of photography in artistic heritage.

When the Tate Gallery opened in 1897 British painters, including Turner, appeared there. The Tate, beside The Thames, now holds the national collection of British art from the 16th century to the present day, as well as an extensive collection of international 20th century art. The restaurant walls are decorated by Rex Whistler and Henry Moore bronzes are in the grounds, outside. The British Museum's supreme collection was based on the will of Sir Hans Sloane in 1753, which prodded Parliament to acquire his art, antiquities and natural history collections at a sum (£ 20,000) far below their actual value. At the same time the Harleian Collection of Manuscripts

Background. British Museum. Facade.

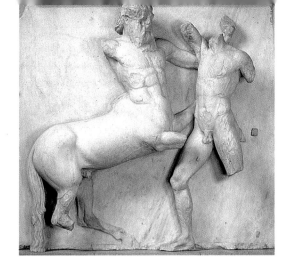

was purchased for the nation and on January 15, 1759 the new museum opened but only to persons considered acceptable. The King's Library was built in 1823 and new wings followed. So did a round Reading Room under a vast copper dome. Ancient works of art abound from Roman hoards unearthed in recent years to copies of the Magna Carta, Parthenon sculptures and Egyptian mummies.

The Victoria and Albert Museum, Science and Natural History Museums in South Kensington grew out of Prince Albert's Great Exhibition initiatives. The V & A, with its fine and applied art, halls of sculpture and costume, came to South Kensington in 1857 with the active support of the Prince. A new building was commissioned forty years later and Queen Victoria laid the foundation stone in 1899 in one of her last public engagements. Statues of the Queen and her Consort are above the ornate main entrance to this treasure house packed with priceless items from jewels to historic costumes to works of art from around the world and British furniture including the giant Bed of Ware, large enough to sleep a whole family.

Victoria & Albert Museum.

Natural History Museum.

A WAY OF LIFE

Covent Garden. Tuttons Bar.

Trocadero.

The Royal Wedding.

Entrance to the Underground.

Telephone booths.

The London Dungeon.

Street signs.

Souvenir stall at Lambeth.

London Beatles Store.   *London Police.*   *New Scotland Yard.*

SHOPPING

Christmas lights in Oxford Street.

Harrods, Knightsbridge.

Burlington Arcade.

Burlington Arcade Interior.

Selfridges, Oxford Street.
The Queen of Time.

Fortnum & Mason. Emblem.

C.D. Harrod, Grocer, was the sign put up by Charles Digby Harrod in 1861, soon after taking over a small retail business from his father. Business prospered and by 1880 staff numbered 100. Disaster struck in December 1883 when the store he had built up for 20 years was engulfed in flames. But Mr Harrod, being a man of determination, sent carriages in all directions to replenish stock in time for Christmas and his customers remained so loyal that trade during that festive season broke records. Actresses Lily Langtry and Ellen Terry were among the first approved customers granted limited credit.

Today Harrods is among the world's best known shops - able to supply anything from a grand piano to a spa treatment for your pet. While this store is synonymous with Knightsbridge, Selfridges, founded by the American Henry Gordon Selfridge in 1909, has Oxford Street's most elaborate facade, incorporating a clock with a figure named the Queen of Time.

An older establishment with royal connections - Fortnum and Mason - was founded in the early 18th century. Its clock is worth watching on the hour when the animated figures of the two founders appear above the Piccadilly frontage, turn and bow to each other. A few paces away is the thoroughfare of the beau monde of the 1980s, Bond Street, with its exclusive fashion shops, fine sil-

ver and Sotheby's, the auction house which opened in 1744, since when it has sold priceless treasures. Items for sale can be inspected a day or two before they come under the hammer.

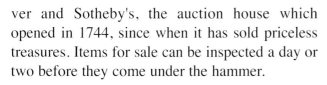

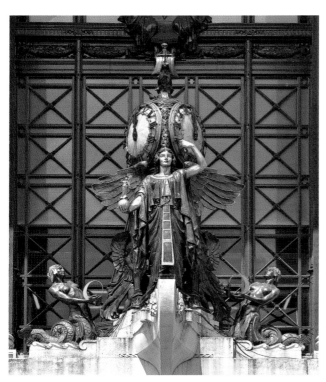

The old and the new double-decker bus.

Taxi.

Bus and underground services, within a radius of about 15 miles from Charing Cross, come within the responsibilities of London Regional Transport, based in offices above the underground at St. James's Park. But the place to study London Transport history is in Covent Garden where the Museum covers nearly two centuries, even before the Omnibus appeared on the capital's streets in 1829.

The first tram service, also horsedrawn, was begun in 1861, two years before the world's first underground railway, the Metropolitan, opened. In 1870 the Tower Subway was constructed with a tunnel under the River Thames, and 20 years later the first electric tube railway rolled into action: the modern London underground was in its infancy.

The 1970s saw further extensions, with the new Jubilee Line, and the Piccadilly Line lengthened to Heathrow Airport and to Heathrow Terminal 4. The same line is now linked to the new Terminal 5. The Docklands Light Railway serves the Docklands area to the east. The new Overground is also designed to link east London to the Olympic Park. On the bus front, George Shillibeer, who started the initial omnibus service, between Paddington

The Underground.

St Pancras Station.

Green and the Bank of England, was followed by competitors, and by 1850 roof seats appeared. The turn of the century saw the coming of the earliest motor-buses, but the last horsebus wasn't withdrawn until 1916, by which time the tramway had been electrified. They were replaced by trolleybuses, which finally disappeared in 1962. Today single-decker buses operate alongside the more iconic double-deckers.

Waterloo Station.

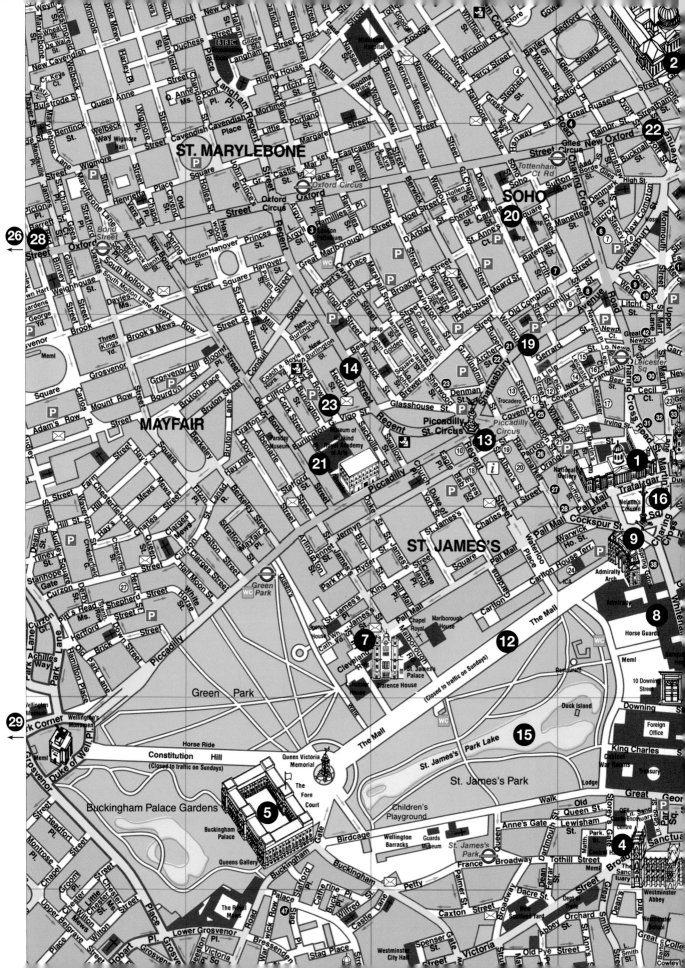

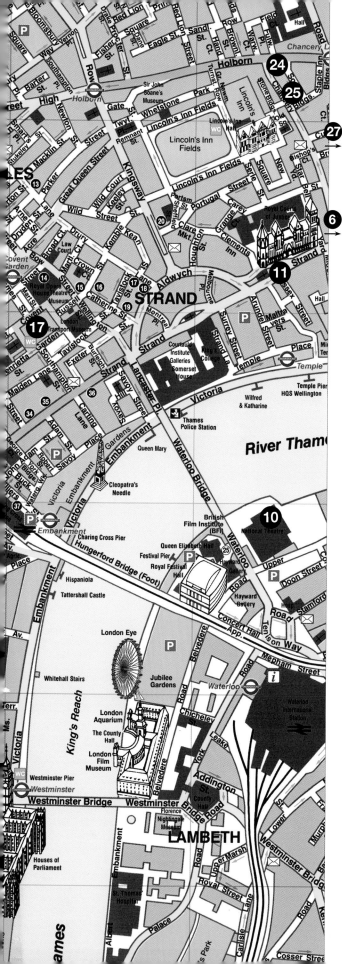

MAP OF CENTRAL LONDON

MAP REFERENCES

ART

1. National Gallery. *Painting*
2. British Museum. *Sculpture*
3. Houses of Parliament. *Decorated Halls*
4. Westminster Abbey. *The British Pantheon*
5. Buckingham Palace. *Royal Palace*
6. St Paul's Cathedral
7. St James's Palace (Henry VIII)

SIGHTS

8. Horse Guards
9. Admiralty Arch
10. National Film Theatre
11. Fleet Street
12. Mall
13. Piccadilly Circus
14. Regent Street
15. St James's Park
16. Trafalgar Square
17. Covent Garden
18. Charing Cross
19. Shaftesbury Avenue
20. Soho

SHOPPING

21. Burlington Arcade
22. Oxford Street
23. Savile Row
24. Diamonds
25. Silver Vaults Chancery Lane
26. Portobello Road
27. Petticoat Lane
28. Selfridges
29. Harrods

Page 64. Westminster and the Houses of Parliament.
Aerial view.